Original title:
The Pear's Wisdom

Copyright © 2025 Creative Arts Management OÜ
All rights reserved.

Author: Julian Carmichael
ISBN HARDBACK: 978-1-80586-435-6
ISBN PAPERBACK: 978-1-80586-907-8

Leafy Lessons

In a garden green with cheer,
Leaves converse, their gossip clear.
One says, "Don't hang too low,
Or the kids will steal your glow!"

While another, slightly wise,
Chimes in with some bright skies:
"Stay plump, and wear your charms,
Or they'll just squeeze you with their arms!"

Time in the Orchard

In the orchard, time does tease,
Fruitful laughter in the breeze.
Carts roll by with distant clang,
As the ripe ones boast and hang.

With every tick, a joke is cracked,
Old trunks sway, their roots intact.
"Life's a game of juice and seed,
Pick your battles, take the lead!"

Juiciness of Thought

In the sun, ideas blend,
Squeezed out thoughts, that never end.
A zesty vibe rolls in the air,
Tasting dreams without a care.

Sour moments can surprise,
Sweet relief in clever guise.
For every squirt of witty jest,
Brings a chuckle, never rest!

Wisdom Carved in Flesh

Carved with humor, oh so bright,
Each bruise tells a funny flight.
"Learn to roll with every fall,
A little squish, that's not so small!"

The laughter echoes through the skin,
Jests and jabs, a joyful din.
Wear your colors, let them show,
For wisdom's juicy, don't you know?

Orchard's Oaths

In the orchard where they gather,
Fruits discuss their juicy chatter.
"I'm ripe," said one with a grin,
"I swear I'll never let you in!"

The apples roll their eyes in jest,
"You think you're good? Just take a rest!"
Pear says, "I'm the one they choose,
But in this game, I just might lose!"

Sweetness of Experience

Oh sweet fruits in the sunny ray,
They share their tales in a funny way.
"I once was green, all tart and tough,
Now I'm sweet; this life is rough!"

A cherry giggles with a twist,
"I once got picked and nearly missed!"
"But here I am, just look at me,
The queen of jams, can't you see?"

A Bough of Understanding

On a bough where laughter swings,
A pear recounts the weirdest things.
"I thought I'd be a star in pies,
But here I am—oh, what a surprise!"

The plums all chuckle, rolling near,
"You think you're great? Oh have no fear!"
"With all your wisdom, try again!
After all, we're just fruit—amen!"

Ripe with Understanding

In a garden where laughter blooms,
Fruits giggle under the bright moon.
They whisper tales of sunny glee,
As branches sway, wild and free.

A ripe one fell with a hearty thud,
'Why not roll down, join the mud?'
Others snicker, 'Oh, what a sight!',
'A coddled fruit, lacking in fright!'

The Orchard's Secrets

In the orchard, secrets abound,
With fruit gossiping all around.
"I'm sweeter than honey," one boast,
As bees swirl in a nectar toast.

A grumpy apple pipes in, "You jest!
I'm crisp and shiny, I'm the best!"
But the kiwi chuckles, "You're all so rude,
We should unite, let's form a food!"

Burdens of the Branches

Branches groan beneath their load,
Complaining of the sweet abode.
"I'm tired of balancing these fruits divine,
Next year, I'll just plant some wine!"

Berries murmur, 'Take a break,
We won't spill if you just shake!'
The tree replies, with careful care,
"Next year, I'll grow a light affair!"

Multitudes of Flavor

Upon a table, colors collide,
With flavors bursting, side by side.
"What's your essence?" asks the zest,
"I'm tangy enough to be the best!"

Lemon laughs, "I'm a summer dream,
Without me, life's just a bland theme!"
"Let's mix it up!" the peach suggests,
And they all cheer, "That's the taste test!"

Lessons from the Leaf

A leaf once said to a bright young sprout,
"Don't rush to grow up, stand tall and shout!"
With laughter, the wind tickled their ears,
As they danced 'round in the joy of their years.

"Stay green and quirky, embrace the strange,
Life's a wild ride, get ready to change!"
With every twist and a turn they'd unveil,
The fun in being just slightly off-scale.

Harvest Moon Wisdom

Beneath a glow from the moon so round,
A jovial fruit party broke new ground.
"Pick me! I'm ripe, and I know what's cool!"
Said an apple who thought he ruled the school.

A pear chuckled loud, "Don't be such a brat,
We're all unique, now how about that?"
With laughter and puns under the sky's dome,
They celebrated their quirks, feeling right at home.

Ripening Realizations

A berry turned soft, sighed with delight,
"Being a fruit gives me quite the height!"
With dreams of sweet jams and gourmet hall,
They laughed at the thought of a fruit-friends ball.

But wisdom came slow, like the sun's warm grace,
Understanding that ripening's not a race.
Instead, they embraced their time in the sun,
Finding joy in each moment—oh, it was fun!

Wisdom from the Garden Path

On a winding path lined with veggies so bright,
A squirrel proposed, "Let's party tonight!"
But carrots, they fretted, "Too many to munch!"
Zucchinis rejoiced, "I say, bring the crunch!"

With laughter and giggles, the garden did sway,
They learned that life's better when fun's here to stay.
So they feasted on jokes, and shared silly tales,
In the heart of the garden, where joy never fails.

Insights in the Shade

Under leafy green, I spy,
A fruit that's round and oh-so spry.
It whispers secrets, bold and bright,
To munch or not? That is the plight.

See it sway with every breeze,
Ripe with laughter, keen to tease.
A burst of joy with every bite,
A treasure found, oh what a sight!

Sweet Truths from the Tree

Hang on tightly, fruit so sweet,
With juicy tales that can't be beat.
A twist of fate or sly maneuver,
Each flavor's dance is quite the groover.

When life gets tough and times are sour,
Find your humor, find your power.
Like a fruit that knows its place,
Just roll with laughter; that's the grace.

The Wisdom of Ripeness

On branches high, a lesson hangs,
A laugh emerges, bright and strong.
To age is wise, or so it seems,
Just plump and bursting with sweet dreams.

When day is done, and night is near,
Don't fear the dark; embrace the cheer.
For in good company, there's bliss,
Each ripple echoes, "Don't you miss!"

Seeded Knowings

In every seed a tale is spun,
Each little story is full of fun.
So plant your thoughts, let laughter grow,
With roots so deep, it's quite the show.

A funny crunch, a silly grin,
Life's simple joys we find within.
So let's gather 'round, take a bite,
And toast to laughter, day and night!

Nature's Reflections

In the orchard where the fruit doth shine,
A squirrel pauses, thinking it's divine.
With each little nibble, he'll surely learn,
That ripe temptation's a tricky turn.

Leaves rustle softly, like gossiping friends,
Nature chuckles as the humor extends.
A bird on a branch, with a cheeky cheer,
Sings to the breeze, 'Life's just a pear!'

Harvested Perspectives

Beneath the sun, the apples roll,
While pears just lounge, taking their toll.
'Why rush?' one says with a playful grin,
'When sweet, juicy laughter is where we begin.'

A rabbit hops by in chase of a dream,
But the wise old pear just claims, 'Let them scheme.'
Life's not just racing from tree to tree,
It's savoring moments, just let it be!

Juicy Contemplations

With every drop of morning dew,
The fruits are giggling, 'What's next to do?'
One apple remarked, 'I'm all about looks!'
While a pear just smiles, 'Let's read some books!'

A worm in the apple, plotting his fate,
Squeezed in the fruit, but never late.
He winks at the rest, 'Life's a grand prank,'
As nature just laughs at the fruit bowl's rank!

Sweet Lessons from Nature

The harvest season struts with flair,
Trees sway in rhythm, without a care.
'What's ripe is more fun,' the branches declare,
While shadows dance lightly, pulling each pair.

A wise old fig shared tales of delight,
While berries beside him sparked merry insight.
Nature's full of quirks, and oh such wit,
Let's laugh at the lessons, and enjoy every bit!

A Symphony of Sweetness

In the orchard where jesters play,
Fruits gossip in their fruity way.
A grape said, 'I'm the star tonight!'
While apples chuckle, holding tight.

Bananas slide, looking for fame,
Pineapples grinning, playing the game.
Lemons complain, 'We're sour, alas!'
But they all laugh as sweetness amasses.

When the wind hums a fruity tune,
Ripe berries dance beneath the moon.
A melon trips, causing a scene,
As laughter swells, oh what a dream!

Underneath the leafy shade,
A fruit salad masquerade.
With every bite, joy takes flight,
In this fruity world, all feels right.

Time's Tender Offering

Once a fruit told tales so grand,
Of all the things that time had planned.
A tick-tock spoke with a fruity twist,
'Life's just a dance, you can't resist!'

Citrus clocks tick tocking bright,
Chasing moments, pure delight.
The fig rolled by in a fancy shoe,
Said, 'Time's just a fruit, enjoy the brew!'

Juggling oranges, so full of zest,
Tangerines joined in, they're the best.
A toast with juice, life's sweet reward,
So grab a glass, and let's not be bored!

With laughter ringing, and juice in hand,
Time become a fruit-filled band.
So sip, savor, and never pout,
For life's a party, we laugh it out!

Guiding through the Branches

In a garden of giggles, under bright skies,
A wise watermelon starts to rise.
'Follow me up this bouncy route,'
He chuckles, 'No time for a pout!'

Bouncing berries trail right behind,
Each twist and turn, oh look what we find!
A fruit parade, with no need to rush,
Bananas slip and giggle with a hush.

Through leafy lanes, they leap and play,
Finding joy in their fruity way.
A catchy tune fills the vibrant air,
With every bounce, they dance without care.

So join this path of fruity fun,
With silly tricks, they've just begun.
As laughter echoes through branches wide,
You'll find wisdom on this joyful ride!

The Aroma of Revelation

Amidst the scents of ripe delight,
Fruits concoct a secret quite light.
A whiff of laughter fills the air,
Strawberries wink with a fruity flair.

Persimmons share tales of cozy nights,
While berries chatter about their flights.
With scents that tease and scents that sway,
They giggle and chuckle, come what may!

In this fruity garden, aromas dance,
In every whiff, there's a chance.
To smell the joy of seasons past,
Where laughter lingers, and friendships last.

So take a breath, let flavors rise,
In the fruity truth, wisdom lies.
With every scent, a story unfolds,
Filled with laughter, more precious than gold.

Orchard of Enlightenment

In the orchard where quirks bloom,
Laughter echoes, dispelling gloom.
Fruit-baskets filled with insights sweet,
Each bite leads to a funny feat.

Beneath the branches, secrets swirl,
Giggles flit like a dancing girl.
Wisdoms planned with a twist of zest,
Come share your snacks, we love a jest!

Silly thoughts like apples fall,
Tasting joy in this tree-crown hall.
Each fruit tells a tale, quite absurd,
Join us here and spread the word!

So pluck your lessons, taste the fun,
In this place, wisdom is never done.
With every crunch and every grin,
Life is sweeter when we begin!

Beneath the Skin's Surface

Beneath the skin, a giggle thrives,
Where fruit-smooth thoughts have wild lives.
Peeling back layers, none too serious,
Just juicy laughs, always curious.

A fruit's interior, oh what a show,
With wobbly seeds all in a row.
Tasting wisdom like custard delight,
Who knew the inside could be so bright?

As we munch, the giggles grow,
Nibbles of knowledge, oh what a flow!
This fruity journey, so light and free,
Peel back more layers, come laugh with me!

So delve into skins, taste their charm,
Each crumb of wisdom keeps us warm.
In this orchard where joy's our game,
Every stitch of humor has its fame!

Harvested Harmony

Harvest time, oh what a spree,
Baskets brim with glee and esprit.
Each pluck of fruit, a joke on hand,
In this garden, laughter's the brand.

As we gather, the banter flows,
Each fruit a tale, a giggle grows.
Squishy jokes, nice and ripe,
Finding fun in every type.

Witty whispers ride the breeze,
Tales of mischief brought to knees.
Harmony found in sour and sweet,
Together we dance, skip, and repeat.

So lift a fruit, toast to the fun,
In harvest season, we're never done.
Gather 'round for a crunchy cheer,
In this orchard, joy is crystal clear!

The Crunch of Clarity

Crunchy bites bring light to mind,
Each munch revealing gems to find.
Silly snacks with a cheeky twist,
In every embed, a giggle kissed.

A nibble offers clarity bright,
Every crunch sends darkness to flight.
Jokes and puns packed in each core,
Eat your fruit, then laugh some more!

Juicy revelations, shimmers of fun,
With every slice, we're already spun.
Munching on knowledge, please take a seat,
Eating up wisdom is quite a treat!

So grab a fruit, hear the sound,
Laughter erupts from the joy around.
With every bite, we sharpen our view,
Finding clarity in this quirky brew!

Nature's Counsel

In the orchard, fruit does spell,
With a grin, the apples yell,
'Life is sweet, just take a bite,
Or you might just lose the fight.'

The berries giggle when they grow,
'We are small, but watch us glow!
If you fall, don't take the blame,
Just sit back and play the game.'

Nuts are laughing, what a show,
'The oak tree sways, just let it go!
Dance in circles, sing out loud,
Join the fun; it's fruit, not crowd!'

So heed the fruits in their green coat,
In laughter, they will surely float,
Take a second, taste the cheer,
And let your worries disappear!

Echoes of Green

In the garden, giggles bloom,
Leaves whisper tales, dispel the gloom,
'Swing from branches, don't be shy,
The grass will catch you, oh my, my!'

Cucumbers dream of being kings,
Debating if they have wings,
'With a pickle or a salad,
We're the brightest, never pallid!'

Mushrooms chuckle in the shade,
Plotting pranks, but never jade,
'Who will poke us first, you think?
They'll trip, we'll giggle, wink and blink!'

So wander where the flowers jest,
In green escapes, you'll find your best,
With every step, let laughter grow,
And send your worries to the flow!

Enlightenment in Bloom

Flowers dance in vibrant hues,
Trading secrets, sharing views,
'Petals whisper, sassy and bright,
Life is funny, hold on tight!'

Daisies suggest a merry prank,
'Count your laughs, not dreams to bank,
With every giggle, life's a feast,
Join the joy; come laugh, at least!'

Sunflowers nod with cheerful glee,
'Look at bees, they're wild and free,
Buzz and twirl, then sip your tea,
For happiness grows in harmony!'

So seek the blooms, in laughter's spree,
They'll guide you on, just wait and see,
With every color, wisdom beams,
And life becomes the best of dreams!

The Orchard's Teachings

In the orchard, folks unite,
With mellow fruits, they share delight,
'Life's a joke, so take a laugh,
Or you'll miss out on the craft!'

Peaches giggle at the risk,
'Be a fool, but in sweet brisk,
Watch your friends slip on the muck,
Just laugh it off, oh what luck!'

Cherries tease in tarty thrill,
Telling tales of capers still,
'Life's too short for serious woes,
Turn each pit into a rose!'

So stroll the lanes with joy uplift,
In the laughter, find your gift,
With fruits abound and jests so ripe,
Harvest joy, it's worth the hype!

Serenity in Simplicity

In orchards bright, where laughter grows,
The fruit hangs low, and everyone knows,
A simple bite, a giggle too,
Life's lessons found in amber hue.

With every crunch, we pause to think,
Juicy truths spilled in a wink,
Nature's joke, so light and sweet,
Finding joy in every bite we eat.

Beneath the tree, we sit in glee,
As squirrels plot their antics, you'll see,
Wisdom wrapped in peel so bright,
A playful twist to nature's light.

So let's rejoice, and squeal with delight,
For simple things make wrongs feel right,
In the orchard, laughter's free,
Life's simplest gifts, just you and me.

Epiphanies in Bloom

In blooms so bright, ideas sprout,
A funny thought, a cheerful shout,
Petals whisper secrets, quite absurd,
A flower's tale is truly heard.

Bees buzzing tales of love and fun,
As nature plays under the sun,
A frolic here, a dance to there,
Every blossom has a quirky flair.

With colors bright, they start to tease,
Why does a bumblebee wear stripes like these?
Their buzzing laugh, a jokester's tune,
In gardens where we laugh with the moon.

So come and frolic, let's bloom with glee,
Discover absurdities sprinkled like tea,
In every petal, a funny rhyme,
Life's absurdities, oh how sublime!

The Heart of Nature's Gift

Beneath the branches, shadows play,
Nature's humor comes out to sway,
A wandering bug with a funny gait,
Tickles the leaves, oh, what a fate!

The fruits all chuckle as they dangle low,
Telling stories of seeds they sow,
A cheeky raccoon in the depths of night,
Stealing snacks in a comical fright.

The wind whispers jokes to the rustling grass,
As trees nod along; they've learned, alas,
That laughter thrives where life's embraced,
Nature's gift is joy interlaced.

So let us roam in this funny land,
Where sunsets joke and waves are grand,
With nature's heart, we find our way,
In funny moments, we laugh and play.

Seeds of Reflection

In tiny seeds, a world does spin,
Planted dreams where giggles begin,
Sprouting thoughts, both wild and free,
Laughter dances in every tree.

Peculiar plants in hues so bright,
Whispering wonders day and night,
The garden's jest, a funny sight,
Where roots tell tales of sheer delight.

With each new sprout, a chuckle grows,
Reflecting life in blissful throes,
Nature's mirror, oh how it gleams,
In silly moments, we find our dreams.

So gather 'round, all ye who roam,
In every garden, you'll find a home,
With seeds of joy that sprout and sing,
A funny dance in life's grand spring.

Harvest of Insight

In the orchard, birds do sing,
A fruit that might just be a king.
What's found inside, so sweet and round,
Could flip your thoughts upside down.

Pulling at branches, oh what a sight!
One slipped and fell, oh what a fright!
The juiciest secrets in every bite,
Brought some wisdom and pure delight.

The squirrels are chattering, what do they know?
About life's lessons, those leaves that blow.
With tree roots deep, they dance and sway,
Teaching us all to play, play, play!

So gather 'round and munch away,
The jokes on fruits that brighten the day.
For in each crunch, you might perceive,
A slice of laughter, if you believe!

The Fruit of Reflection

In a basket full of yellow glow,
Lies a fruit with much to show.
Its shape may puzzle, some may pout,
But wisdom hides, without a doubt.

Oh, pluck it gently, with great care!
Would it tell secrets? What a flair!
A giggle escapes as it rolls away,
Who knew a fruit could be so play?

Gather 'round, friends, let's have some fun,
With witty thoughts, we'll weigh a ton!
Insider jokes, they seem to sprout,
With every bite, we laugh and shout!

So take a moment, just pause and munch,
In every flavor, there's a punch.
The fruit of life, so rich and sweet,
Teaches us joy in every treat!

Lessons from the Grove

Under the leaves, a wise one sits,
Giggling softly with tiny fits.
What can we learn in this leafy den?
Life's pretty quirky, again and again.

One day a bird tried to be sly,
Swiped a fruit, oh my, oh my!
It tumbled down, made quite the mess,
But laughter reigned, nothing less!

The wise old tree simply chuckled loud,
With branches swaying, it felt so proud.
For every wobble is a tale to share,
In the grove of life, joy is everywhere!

So heed the lessons as they unfold,
In every fruit, a story told.
With laughter and smiles, we will find,
That wisdom's ripe, in heart and mind!

Ripe Thoughts

Oh, the branches are bowing low,
With fruits of knowledge all in a row.
Each one whispers a giggling tease,
Tickling thoughts with delightful ease.

With every bite, a chuckle starts,
Through fruity riddles, it warms our hearts.
The juiciest themes, so utterly bright,
Bring silly grins, from day to night.

Rolling down hills, they splash in the mud,
Creating puddles of wisdom, oh what a flood!
Let's gather 'round, there's fun to be had,
In every misstep, we're just a tad mad!

So cheers to the moments, light as a breeze,
Where laughter's the fruit that grows with ease.
Embrace life's quirks and let spirits soar,
For wisdom is ripe, forevermore!

Parables of the Orchard

In the orchard where fruit flies,
A chatty pear taught me to rise.
With jellybeans under a tree,
She said, "Life's sweet, just let it be!"

Squirrels dance, and birds swoop low,
Laughing at troubles, all aglow.
"Don't stew over a pit that's sour,
Just grow roots, and bloom like a flower!"

A bouncing peach chimed in with flair,
"Life's a patchwork; don't you dare!
Mix colors bright, and paint the day,
With laughter, joy will always play!"

So I heed the fruity advice,
With giggles galore, it's oh so nice!
In this orchard of dreams so grand,
I find wisdom in the fruit's soft hand.

Golden Drop of Enlightenment

In a sunshine-drenched grove I lay,
A comical fig had much to say.
"Life's a sip of the sweetest juice,
Don't fret too much, just let it loose!"

With blushing cheeks and a twist of zest,
He giggled loud, took humor's quest.
"So many folks take life too serious,
Taste the sunshine; it's all delirious!"

An apple chortled from the next branch,
"Freedom's found in a good old dance!
Twist and shout, let your worries drop,
Life's a party; you can't just stop!"

Underneath the boughs of the wise,
The golden sap turned into surprise.
With laughter echoing in the air,
I learned to play from the fruity flare!

Sage of the Orchard

Amidst the trees, a wise old plum,
Cracked jokes of life; I said, "Oh, yum!"
He chuckled deep, a belly laugh,
"Turn sour days into sweet giraffe!"

The sunbeams danced on ripened fruit,
While rabbits giggled, oh so cute.
"Don't let the worms steal your fun,
When life gets dull, go on the run!"

A jolly cucumber dropped by to chat,
"Keep it fresh, just like your hat!
Chipper cheer is what you need,
Flavors burst when you plant a seed!"

So in this orchard wisdom grows,
With laughter strong as a garden hose.
In each bite of life, taste the jest,
For humor surely beats all the rest!

Whispering Sweetness

Beneath the vines, a soft voice sighed,
A gentle berry, full of pride.
"The secret's simple; just be spry,
Dance through troubles, let worries fly!"

A wobbly banana joined the cheer,
"Slip and fall, but never fear!
Each bruise tells tales of the quest,
With laughter, love will manifest!"

From blossoms bright to thorns on stems,
Life's a puzzle with quirky gems.
Embrace the weird, the funny plight,
In every shadow, find the light!"

So here in nature's grand old show,
I learned to giggle and let joy flow.
With fruits around me, wisdom speaks,
In whispers sweet, for fun it seeks!

Beneath the Green Canopy

In a tree full of giggles, a fruit hangs tight,
Wobbling and swaying, it teases with might.
"Pick me! I'm ripe!" it shouts with a grin,
But get too close, and it might just spin!

Squirrels gather round for a comedy show,
As fruity wisecracks steal the whole show.
With every wild joke, they crack up in trees,
While the golden sun laughs, dancing with ease.

Wisdom in Every Bite

Bite into the bliss with a squeak and a crunch,
Juicy tales spill out, so let's pack a lunch!
With giggles and grins under sun's shining light,
Each slice is a story, oh what a delight!

It whispers of secrets like wisecracking jest,
Taking you places, forget all the rest!
A nibble of knowledge, a chuckle or two,
Who knew that cheap snacks could be wise and so true?

Roots of Understanding

Down in the dirt, where the roots twist and play,
A gathering of veggies shares jokes every day.
"Why did the potato bring a pear to the dance?"
"Because he saw it glimmer, and he fancied a chance!"

Each root has a tale, a quirk or a pith,
Fables of wisdom lie hidden, so myth.
If you dig down deep, what a riddle you'll find,
A laughing bouquet, and it's one of a kind!

Fruition of Thought

In a bowl of bright colors, ideas collide,
A riot of fruits, it's a whimsical ride.
Throw in a couple of jokes, let them stew,
And a marvelous salad of laughter will brew!

The more that you mix, the funnier it gets,
Fruity punchlines, with no real regrets.
So open your mind, taste a pun that ignites,
Life's zesty adventures in every bite!

Whispers of the Wind

In the orchard, secrets sway,
Fruitful gossip day by day.
Leaves giggle in a light, sweet breeze,
While bees hum songs to tease and please.

Laughter ripens on the vine,
With jokes that taste just like good wine.
A twist of fate, a slippery peel,
Makes wisdom chase like a clown's big wheel.

Branches shake with ancient tales,
Of tarts and pies and thorny scales.
Each fruit tells a raucous joke,
As roots chuckle, beneath the cloak.

So gather 'round for laughs profound,
In boughs where wisdom can be found.
The light-hearted truth is full of grace,
As fruits of fun fill up the space.

Intertwined with Knowledge

In the garden of puzzled minds,
Are fruits where laughter freely finds.
Peels of wisdom, tangy zest,
The quirkiest thoughts are surely best.

A jester's cap sits atop a tree,
Whispering secrets, come and see!
The fruits conspire in silent glee,
Filling the air with fruity spree.

One asks, 'What's the ripest line?'
The other grins, 'Life's a sweet design!'
Riddles hang like dusky fruit,
Each answer bounces, nimble and cute.

So pick a fruit, let humor bloom,
In every giggle find the room.
The mixture of joy and silliness,
Sprinkles the garden with blissful mess.

Abundant Revelations

The air is thick with juicy hoots,
Where apples spin in silly boots.
Mirth drips off the jumbled vines,
As wisdom dances in funny lines.

Underneath the twinkling sky,
Truths hang low, and glares are spry.
One fruit exclaims, 'I'm the best to taste!'
While others roll with a fruity haste.

This fruit's too ripe for a serious chat,
Witty one-liners that make you splat!
A splash of laugh in every slice,
They poke fun at life, oh so nice!

Plucking giggles from leafy threads,
As wisdom's wine fills our heads.
So toast to humor, laughter's gain,
In this orchard, joy is the main course, no pain.

In the Shade of Understanding

Beneath the boughs, wise jokes unfold,
Where radiant humor, never old.
Each twist of fate is a punchline bright,
That tickles the ears and ignites delight.

Fruits of laughter swing and drop,
Bouncing jests until we stop.
In every shade, a jest awakes,
As memories swirl like fruit cake mixes.

One chuckles, 'Why did the fruit cross?',
'To get to the juice, or so it toss!'
In wit's embrace, we find the sun,
And taste the fun when day is done.

So nestle down, let humor reign,
In fruity groves, there's joy to gain.
With each ripe bite, we swap a grin,
In the shade of fun, all can win.

Melodies of Mellow

In the orchard, laughter flows,
With juicy tales of friend and foe.
A fruit that winks with every bite,
It sings of life, oh what a sight!

When life gets tough, just take a snack,
Let sweetness guide you on the track.
Beneath the shade, we dance and sway,
With fruity tunes to bright our day.

There's wisdom found in every core,
A twist of fate we can't ignore.
So let us share a fruity jest,
And raise a toast, we are the best!

In every slice, a giggle hides,
As flavor swirls and joy abides.
So join the fun, don't hesitate,
Let's feast on fruit and celebrate!

Beneath the Green Canopy

Under leafy roofs we meet,
The air is sweet, oh what a treat!
We joke with fruits, they chuckle back,
In this green world, we've got the knack!

Conversations roll like a ripe good pear,
With laughter dancing in the air.
Beneath the boughs, we swing and sway,
The wisdom shared—come join the play!

A pear-shaped joke can turn the frown,
With every bite, the smiles abound.
So take a seat, under the spread,
Let's crunch and munch, no need for dread!

The canopy holds, our giggles soar,
A fruity feast, who could ask for more?
In laughter's shade, let's take a chance,
Life is sweeter with a pear-shaped dance!

The Study of Sweetness

In class we sit, our snacks in hand,
Discussing fruit from every land.
A juicy lecture on the zest,
Where laughter wins and taste is best!

The quizzes here are filled with cheer,
What's the best? It's crystal clear!
With giggles swirling, minds ignite,
The sweetest fruit is such a delight!

We ponder over flavors and crunch,
With every question comes a munch.
In study halls, we spread the bliss,
Each fruity bite, a hug and kiss!

The test of life, it seems so fair,
With humor wrapped in juicy care.
So grab a bite, don't think too hard,
The study here is never marred!

Seeds of Reflection

In gardens rich, we plant our dreams,
With playful thoughts and joyful beams.
The seeds we sow may not be straight,
But who needs rules when you have fate?

We watch in awe as fruits appear,
Each one a tale, a laugh, a cheer.
The quirky shapes and colors bright,
Bring smiles and joy, what pure delight!

As we reflect on life's sweet jest,
The quirks we share, it's all the best.
In fruity realms, we laugh and play,
Where wisdom grows, come what may!

Let's share a slice, let's break the crust,
In every bite, we place our trust.
With seeds of laughter, hearts align,
In life's great fruit bowl, we all shine!

Verdant Whispers

In a garden, green and bright,
Beneath the sun, such a sight,
Whispers of fruit, oh so sly,
"Don't rush, my friend, just stand by."

Round and plump, a fruit so bold,
Tales of sweetness, or so I'm told,
"Patience," it giggles, "That's the key,
Too soon, my friend, and you'll just see!"

A pluck of pride, and off it goes,
With a pop, like a clown's nose,
Juices flowing, laughter bright,
"Now, that's the magic of delight!"

So heed the call of nature's jest,
Life's silly moments, they're the best,
In fields of green, where laughter stirs,
The funny ways of earthly blurs.

The Nectar of Life

A fruit that hangs from branches high,
Tells a joke as the winds pass by,
"Pick me soon, or I'll explode,
Juicy laughter on your road!"

Sipping nectar, a sweet delight,
A taste that dances, day and night,
"Who needs a drink when you have me?
I'm all the fun you'll ever need!"

With every munch, a chuckle flows,
The more you eat, the sillier it goes,
"Spill a bit, and you'll wear a grin,
Life's too short, so dig right in!"

In orchards vast, where jokes abound,
Fruits of laughter tumble down,
Nature's nectar, oh what a thrill,
A sip or two, and you're quite ill!

Wisdom's Harvest

Under branches, shadows dance,
Fruits of laughter, take a chance,
"Wisdom comes, but in small bites,
So laugh away on summer nights!"

Round and yellow, they like to tease,
"Pick me, eat me, if you please!
But mind your manners, what's the plan?
Strange things happen if you can!"

So grab a seat, stay for a while,
Giggling fruits will make you smile,
"A harvest ripe with silly cheer,
Join our fun, we hold it dear!"

With every nibble, giggles spread,
Fruits, they know, what lies ahead,
In the orchard's play, they find delight,
Wisdom's harvest, oh what a sight!

Nature's Epiphany

In a field of whims, a secret grows,
A round delight in nature's clothes,
"Too perfect for the common hand,
Embrace the silliness, understand!"

A fruit that rolls when touched just right,
Spinning tales with all its might,
"Catch me if you can, oh dear friend,
Grin while you chase, around the bend!"

As laughter bursts like morning sun,
Nature shows us, we're all having fun,
"Jump and skip, let spirits fly,
In this dance, we'll never die!"

So heed the call of nature's spree,
Find joy in fruit, your heart will see,
Nature's epiphany, bright and clear,
Life's a joke, so let's all cheer!

Tastes of Time's Fare

In the orchard, fruit does sway,
Beneath the sun's warm, golden ray.
When life hands you a juicy pear,
Make sure you handle with great care!

Slicing through, the juice does fly,
Wipe your chin, oh me, oh my!
Each bite tickles, sweet and neat,
But seeds are tricky, mind your seat!

A dance with flavor, quirky fun,
Giggling with friends, we weigh a ton.
Chasing laughter, we're all fools,
Just watch the tree, it holds the rules!

So let's rejoice in this great feast,
For nature's bounty, to say the least.
With every crunch, life feels so right,
Taste the day, it's pure delight!

Orchard Meditations

In a grove where giggles roam,
The fruit speaks wisdom, who needs a tome?
A plump one winks, a sly surprise,
I hear the laughs in nature's guise.

The apples fretting, fearing fate,
Pears just chuckle, it's never too late.
A fruit debate beneath the sun,
Who's juicier? Let the games be fun!

Leaves whisper jokes in summer's breeze,
Pondering life from boughs with ease.
Hilarity in each summer's glow,
Turns ripe discussions into a show.

So grab your friends, it's harvest time,
Join the laughter, it's truly sublime.
In this orchard of jocular cheer,
The lessons come, loud and clear!

Lessons from the Harvest Moon

Beneath the glow of a laughing moon,
We gather fruit, we swoon and croon.
With baskets full, our spirits soar,
Chasing critters we can't ignore!

The raccoons dance, plot their scheme,
Stealing snacks, or is it a dream?
As we chuckle, they just stare,
A game of wit, oh how unfair!

In the twilight, we tell our tales,
Of fruits and pies and stormy gales.
Each bite a memory, sweet and wide,
Where laughter meets the evening tide.

So in the glow, our hearts will bloom,
Harvesting joy outside the gloom.
With every chuckle and playful jest,
Nature's bounty surely is the best!

Nature's Gentle Counsel

In the garden, wisdom flows,
From plants that giggle as they grow.
A cucumber grins, so fresh and keen,
While broccoli dons a leafy green.

"Be fruity," says the bouncing pear,
"Life's too short for heavy wear."
With each crop under the sunlit sky,
It's clear we're meant to laugh and fly.

Tomatoes blush, they're shy but bold,
In nature's tales, the secrets told.
Lettuce whispers in the breeze,
Bouncing wisdom with such ease!

So take a stroll through this rowdy patch,
And let the humor be your catch.
With nature's counsel, life's a jest,
Join the frolic, it's simply the best!

The Branch's Teachings

In the orchard high, a great debate,
Boughs arguing of fruit, in funny fate.
"Who's juicier?" one cried, with zest and cheer,
"That's my spot!" another barked, feeling sheer.

Leaves shook with laughter, a rustling sound,
As squirrels gathered 'round, making jokes abound.
"Look at that one!" they jested with glee,
"He's just a stick, thinking he's a tree!"

Twisting in breezes, the branches would sway,
Holding their laughter, through night and day.
"Hey, don't hang your head, your time will come!"
Each knot and curve knew fruit would soon hum.

So as they jostled, the sun stood still,
Each branch learned well, a lesson to thrill.
Laughter is ripe when you share it right,
Mirth in the orchard, a pure delight!

Cultivating Clarity

Planting ideas, a quirky old seed,
In time it would sprout, fulfilling a need.
"Growth takes patience!" the gardener sighed,
As weeds danced around, all sprightly and wide.

Sunshine wrapped thoughts in a golden embrace,
While rainclouds joked, splashing smiles on the face.
"Need a good laugh?" they would often ask,
"Just look for a fruit with an unusual mask!"

Rooted in humor, the garden would thrive,
Each laugh sowed seeds; the joy kept alive.
"You're just like a fruit, be silly and sweet!"
The veggies would cheer as they shared a treat.

So when the harvest came, all hearty and bright,
The turnips wore hats, a comical sight.
In the field where clarity found a way,
Laughter and joy flourished every day!

Harmony in the Orchard

In an orchard of giggles, the fruits convened,
Ripe bursts of joy in colors that beamed.
"Hey, let's harmonize!" the apples declared,
"Before the wind's tune leaves us all quite scared!"

Bananas chimed in, with a slip and a slide,
"Let's shake up the branches, we'll swing with pride!"
With melodies flowing from trees far and wide,
They danced and they swayed, with laughter as guide.

A choir of citrus, the lemons brought zest,
While cherries clapped hands; truly feeling blessed.
"Join in the fun!" sang the pears in a row,
As laughter erupted; the humor would grow.

So music of fruit filled the bright sunny day,
In a rhythm of joy, they danced and they'd play.
Harmony echoed, bringing life to the trees,
Each fruit found its laughter, flying on the breeze!

Reflections of the Orchard

In the mirror of dew, the orchard did preen,
Reflecting on moments, so funny and keen.
"Look at me shine!" the berries exclaimed,
"With colors so bold, we should all be named!"

The apples were chuckling, big grins on display,
"We're crisp and we're bright, not just another day!"
As shadows continued this humorous play,
They giggled and jostled, come what may.

Dandelions joined in, a sprightly affair,
"With seeds that we spread, let's make it quite rare!"
They whispered their wishes with humorous flair,
"Who knew we could be so light in the air?"

So as twilight fell, reflections in sight,
Laughter rippled through, from morning till night.
In the orchard's bright humor, a shared rendezvous,
With echoes of joy that forever renew!

The Language of Flavor

In the orchard where sweetness sings,
Fruits chatter, wearing heirloom rings.
An apple quipped, 'I'm quite divine!'
While a banana said, 'Your shine is fine!'

A citrus burst, with zesty flair,
Said, 'Life's a salad, if you dare!'
Beneath the leaves, the berries jest,
'Tickle your taste; it's for the best!'

The grapes fell down, in a grape-like way,
'Just blend us in, on any day!'
A melon sang, in a breeze so sweet,
'Join our feast, oh what a treat!'

So many flavors, a fruity crew,
Spreading laughs, and fun—who knew?
In each bite, a giggle waits,
Join the dance, as Nature creates!

Blossom and Know

In the garden where colors bloom,
Petals whisper, dispelling gloom.
'Study the brush of the bee's mad haste,'
Said the rose, with petals laced.

The tulip giggled, bright and bold,
'What stories of beauty are too sweet to hold!'
Lilies chimed in, 'Whiff our perfume,
A scent so grand, it lights the room!'

The sunflowers winked in the gentle breeze,
'Turn to us, and we'll make you tease!'
With a sway of their heads, they play along,
Teaching laughter, in nature's song.

Together they shared their wisdom rare,
'Bloom where you're planted, and just don't care!'
With every giggle, a seed is sown,
In the laughter, true joy is grown!

Nature's Silent Teacher

Underneath the canopy, where shadows play,
Quietly teaching in nature's way.
A squirrel paused, with a cheeky grin,
'Life's a game, come and join in!'

The river chuckled, as it flowed by,
'Splash around, let your worries fly!'
Moss whispered softly, growing wise,
'Listen to the tales that nature supplies.'

A rock rolled by, with a thud so loud,
'Time teaches patience, just feel proud!'
While the trees waved, their branches high,
'We're all connected, just look and try!'

So heed the lessons in silence spun,
With humor and heart, surely fun!
Nature's giggles and quiet shocks,
Take a stroll and explore the docks!

The Tapestry of Taste

In a kitchen full of scents and sights,
Flavors mingled, scaling heights.
Garlic danced with herbs in hand,
As spices swirled like a rock band!

The onions cried, but with glee in tears,
'We make meals tasty over the years!'
Tomatoes blushed, on the counter they lay,
'Add a pinch of fun, make a bouquet!'

Baking powder puffed, 'I rise to the call!'
While sugar giggled, 'I'm the life of the ball!'
Yeast bubbled up, 'Just wait and see,
In doughy embrace, we'll all be free!'

With every stir, a giggle emerged,
From simple ingredients, creativity surged!
In the tapestry, each thread entwined,
A feast of laughter, with flavor aligned!

Whispers of the Grove

In the grove where shadows play,
Fruits wear hats and dance all day.
A pear once told a joke so grand,
The trees all chuckled, what a band!

Squirrels joined in with acorn cheers,
While birds flew close, flapping their gears.
A game of hide and seek was spun,
Oh, the fun beneath the sun!

The ferns would giggle when storms rolled near,
As laughter echoed through each sphere.
With every breeze, a pun took flight,
Grove's merry sounds, a pure delight!

So if you wander, pause a while,
Embrace the joy, let nature smile.
In this grove, wisdom grows anew,
With a sprinkle of laughter, life's a brew!

Nectar of Nurture

In a garden lush with glittered dew,
A bee once hosted a raucous crew.
With nectar sweet and tales to share,
They painted jokes on floating air!

"Why did the bee wear a vest so bright?"
"Because it's buzzing with style tonight!"
Flowers burst with laughter's embrace,
With petals dancing all over the place.

Sunshine giggled, clouds rolled their eyes,
While butterflies spun in comic highs.
The earth spoke in whispered puns,
Each moment spun into merry runs.

Join the frolic, let spirits soar,
Nature's wisdom is never a bore.
In blooming laughter, life's a treat,
Nurtured by joy, it's perfectly sweet!

Ripe Reflections

In a bowl of fruit so snug and round,
A ripe one claimed, "I wear a crown!"
"Who needs a robe when I can shine?"
Others chimed in, "We're all divine!"

An apple blushed, "I'm just as fine,
But your jokes are truly the best line!"
They rolled in laughter, bursting free,
Reflecting joy in unity.

A banana slipped with a goofy grin,
Said, "Peel the fun, let it begin!"
Berries giggled, having a ball,
In their fruit world, they ruled them all!

So here's a toast to fruits so bright,
With wisdom ripe and humor tight.
In this bowl of cheer, let's raise a cheer,
For laughter's essence, forever dear!

The Bounty of Insight

In a market bustling, full and loud,
A fruit stand formed the silliest crowd.
Cherries giggled, "We've got the zest!"
While melons claimed, "Taste us, we're best!"

An orange joked, "I'm feeling fine,
Just cannot stop this peel of mine!"
Lemons chimed in, "We're sour with glee,
But sprinkle some sugar, we're tasty, you'll see!"

As shoppers passed with smiles aglow,
They'd laugh with fruits putting on a show.
"Take me home," said a peach with flair,
"Together we'll spread the joy we share!"

So ponder well, what fruits can teach,
In every laugh, new lessons reach.
With bounty rich and humor bright,
Life's sweetest wisdom starts with light!

Fruits of Experience

In a garden full of cheer,
Where laughter runs quite near,
A fruit named for its round face,
Claims to be the wisest in this place.

With every juicy bite you take,
It shares a smile, for goodness' sake!
"Life's a squeeze!" it seems to say,
"Enjoy the juice, come what may!"

As friends all gather, munching loud,
A grape cried out, feeling proud,
"I've rolled through life with zest and glee,
Yet still, I envy what's so free!"

The wisdom from this fruity crew,
Is often sweet, but sometimes askew;
So heed the laughs and take a chance,
For life's too quick, don't miss the dance!

Pondering Pears

In a bistro filled with gleeful chatter,
A pear was caught in thoughtful matter,
"Why do folks find me so divine?"
"Is it my curve or vintage line?"

An apple scoffed, "You're just a snack!"
"Oh please!" said pear, "Give kindness back!"
"At least I'm not as red as health!"
"And I don't sit upon the shelf!"

A strawberry giggled with a rush,
"You're ripe for fame, but do not hush!"
"Ponder on...but share with glee,
For fruits like us live wild and free!"

With that, they chuckled, memories shared,
Of juicy days when none had cared;
In laughter, wisdom came to light,
Sometimes we're funny—such delight!

Bountiful Reflections

In the orchard's bright embrace,
A pear proclaimed, with high-flying grace,
"Life is juicy, filled with fun!"
"More excitement than a double run!"

Along came a bunch of tart old limes,
"What's the buzz? We have good rhymes!"
"We've rolled the way, through sun and gloom,
Each zesty tale, we'll surely bloom!"

Amidst the banter, a banana grinned,
"I've been peeled back, embraced, and pinned!"
"But wisdom's naught in shying shame,
Every slip leads to glorious fame!"

With giggles bright, the fruits convened,
In their reflection, faces beamed;
That laughter, joy—these harvest yields,
Enriched the soil of life's vast fields!

Gleaning Truths

In the sun where stories clash,
A fruit held court, causing a splash;
"I'm the smoothest in this crowd,
Listen up, I'm feeling proud!"

Beneath the tree, wisdom flowed,
With giggles high, and tales bestowed;
A citrus said, "You are so ripe!"
With all its zest, it made a type!

But then a fig, wise and sage,
Piped up loud from a leafy stage;
"Life's not just sweetness, you must know,
The light grows brighter through the low!"

So they raised their voices, fruit full of cheer,
In their juicy hearts, no need to fear;
For every laugh and tasty quest,
Are gleaned as truths—life's very best!

Shade of Ancient Trees

Underneath old trunks, laughter flows,
Squirrels dance while the sunlight glows.
Branches whisper secrets of days gone by,
Leaves exchange jokes, and the clouds sigh.

A turtle raves about a snail's pace,
"Don't rush!" he chuckles, "It's a long race!"
The wise owl hoots in a comical tone,
"Time flies, but you won't hear it moan!"

A raccoon jests, with a wink of his eye,
"Take life a shade lighter—give it a try!"
Nature's jesters, in their leafy retreat,
Share tales of folly, amusing and sweet.

So settle in close, under branches so grand,
Let laughter and shade go hand in hand.
In this merry place where time bends and sways,
Let the wise trees teach us to play and to play.

Sweetness of Experience

A honeybee buzzes with tales to unfold,
Of nectar and flowers, both spicy and bold.
"Try this," she says, with a grin on her face,
"Life's all about sweetness, so savor your grace!"

A butterfly flutters, all colors aflame,
"Life's just a dance; don't you play the same!"
Spinning in circles, they laugh and then shout,
"Those who don't try—well, they miss out!"

A wise old cat, with a wink from his chair,
Claims chasing his tail is the best kind of dare.
"Experience," he purrs, while giving a yawn,
"Is knowing when to nap and when to carry on!"

So gather your lessons, as life serves its pie,
Don't fear to dig in, just let humor fly.
For sweetness is found in the twists and the turns,
In the laughter of lessons, that everyone learns.

Harvesting Truths

In fields of folly, the scarecrow stands tall,
Plucking up wisdom, for one and for all.
"Why worry?" he muses, "when fun's in the air?
Life's just a harvest of laughter to share!"

A gopher pops up with a grin on his face,
"Roots run deep, just like our disgrace!"
He digs for the truths that the others might miss,
With a wink and a grin, he can't help but hiss.

Chickens all cluck with their snickers and crows,
"Life's like our pecking; it's all in the throws!"
"Take a little risk, and you just might arise,
In fields where the humor always belies!"

So gather your pals as you work in the sun,
Harvesting laughter, it's all in the fun.
From the silly to wise, let your joys intertwine,
And enjoy every moment, for truth's in the vine!

Essence of Earth's Teachings

Amidst the dirt, worms wiggle with glee,
Sharing their secrets, sprightly and free.
"Don't fret," they insist, "the soil knows the way,
Life's a big party, just brighten your day!"

Wind whispers stories that tumble and sway,
"Why worry about clouds? Just dance in the gray!"
A funky old rock chimes in with a nod,
"Let laughter be seeds; see what they've plod!"

So gather your friends at the base of a hill,
Nature's wise creatures, so quirky and chill.
From compost to cosmos, let humor ignite,
In the essence of learning, we laugh day and night.

And when you feel lost, just look to the ground,
The earth, full of wisdom, is all around.
With chuckles and giggles, let the lesson be clear,
It's all about joy—the best kind of cheer!

Juice of Generations

In the orchard where laughter flows,
Golden fruits boast of the wisdom they know.
With each bite, stories swirl and twirl,
Juicy tales from each wrinkled pearl.

Granny claimed her secret so true,
It all started from a tree's lovely view.
But really, she ate too much at brunch,
And didn't share, not even a munch!

Children giggle, pies and cakes abound,
Juices sticking to the silly ground.
With each drop, legacy so divine,
Who knew wisdom could taste so fine?

So gather around under the sun,
With laughter and juice, we all are one.
In this orchard of laughter, come take a stand,
For knowledge tickles when you eat it by hand!

Blossoms of Knowledge

In springtime bloom, wisdom takes flight,
With blossoms so bright, a comical sight.
Each petal whispers, 'Don't overthink!'
The fruit of laughter is the best drink.

Old trees know how to sway and tease,
With winds that tickle, they dance with ease.
Fall might stumble in playful jest,
But tree limbs hold the world's best fest!

Mud pies made from those funny old roots,
Bring cheerful fun, sweet laughs, and hoots.
Why wear boots when you can squish?
Nature's own recipe—silly and swish!

So share the blooms and let laughter rain,
In jokes and jests, there's never much pain.
Harvest merriment, dress up with a smile,
For wisdom grows when we laugh for a while!

Secrets Held in Skin

Underneath the surface, wisdom hides,
In the skin of fruit, each secret abides.
With a peel that crinkles like grandma's hands,
Lies a treasure map to sweet, silly lands.

An apple's a tale of mischief and fun,
While pears just giggle in the warm sun.
Why's the grape always bursting with cheer?
Because it knows how to let go of fear!

Beneath each layer, laughter does thread,
Wrapped in skin, where wit is fed.
So take a bite and take it all in,
The best kind of knowledge makes you grin!

So gather your friends, and share a snack,
Each fruit a story, so come on back!
Grab that fruit salad, it's really a win,
For wisdom's the juice of the giggles within!

Legacy of the Orchard

In the orchard where giggles grow tall,
Each branch a legend, a story for all.
Roots that whisper, 'Don't take life too serious',
For laughter's the key to being mysterious!

Fruits dangling, teasing the hungry crowd,
With a wink and a nudge, they're cheeky and proud.
Grandpa said, 'Squeeze the juice from your days,'
While grandma just chuckled and danced in a haze.

With every bite, bites of joy we glean,
The orchard's a show; it's the fruitiest scene!
Who knew wisdom would come with a crunch?
In laughter and sweetness, we all share a bunch!

So gather 'round, let the stories unwind,
In every fruit, a giggle you'll find.
Orchards of laughter, our legacy bright,
Planted in joy, bringing smiles day and night!

www.ingramcontent.com/pod-product-compliance
Lightning Source LLC
Chambersburg PA
CBHW060129230426
43661CB00003B/367